Making the Past into Presents

Jo Brooker

Heinemann Educational Publishers
Halley Court, Jordan Hill, Oxford OX2 8EJ
a division of Reed Educational & Professional Publishing Limited

Heinemann is a registered trademark of Reed Educational & Professional Publishing Limited

OXFORD MELBOURNE AUCKLAND
JOHANNESBURG BLANTYRE GABORONE
IBADAN PORTSMOUTH (NH) USA CHICAGO

© Reed Educational and Professional Publishing, 1998
The moral right of the proprietor has been asserted.

First published 1998

02 01 00 99
10 9 8 7 6 5 4 3

British Library Cataloguing in Publication Data
A catalogue record for this book is available from the British Library.

ISBN 0 435 09649 4   *Making the Past into Presents* single copy

ISBN 0 435 09650 8   *Making the Past into Presents* 6 copy pack

All rights reserved. No part of this publication may be reproduced or transmitted in any form, or by any means, electronic or mechanical, including photocopy, recording or any information storage and retrieval system without permission in writing from the publishers.

Designed by M2
Printed and bound in the UK

Acknowledgements

Photos
Telegraph Colour Library, cover and page 10. Ronald Sheridan / Ancient Art and Architecture Collection, pages 8 and 16. Brian Wilson / Ancient Art and Architecture Collection, contents page top, page 4 top and page 12. C M Dixon, pages 5 top, 14 and 18. All other photos by Keith Lillis.

Illustrations
Oxford Illustrators, pages 6 and 7.

Models and art direction by Jo Brooker.

Contents

Introduction 4
Ancient civilisations 6
Egyptian necklace 8
Egyptian pyramid 10
Greek coins 12
Greek temple photo frame 14
Roman scroll 16
Roman mosaic draughts board .. 18
Templates 20
Bibliography 23
Index 24

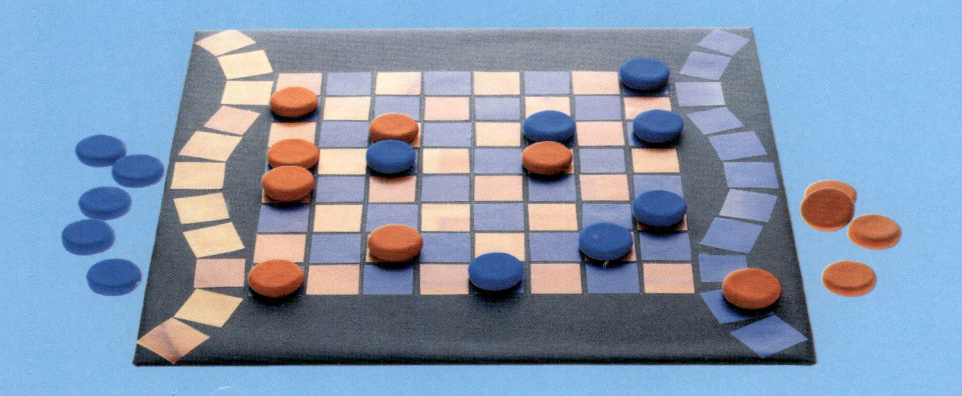

Introduction

The past is all around us. We know about how people in the past lived because many of the things they made and used have been found. From the huge Egyptian pyramids to the smallest piece of Roman pottery, every artefact* tells us something about the civilisation it came from.

Artists and craftspeople have always looked to the past for inspiration. This book shows how you can use artefacts from ancient civilisations for ideas for your own arts and crafts. Step-by-step instructions show how to make Egyptian, Greek or Roman works of art to keep or give away to family and friends. In other words, it shows how to make the past into presents!

* an ornament, tool or other object that is made by people

NO ONE KNOWS UNTIL THEY TRY.

ROMAN QUOTE

5

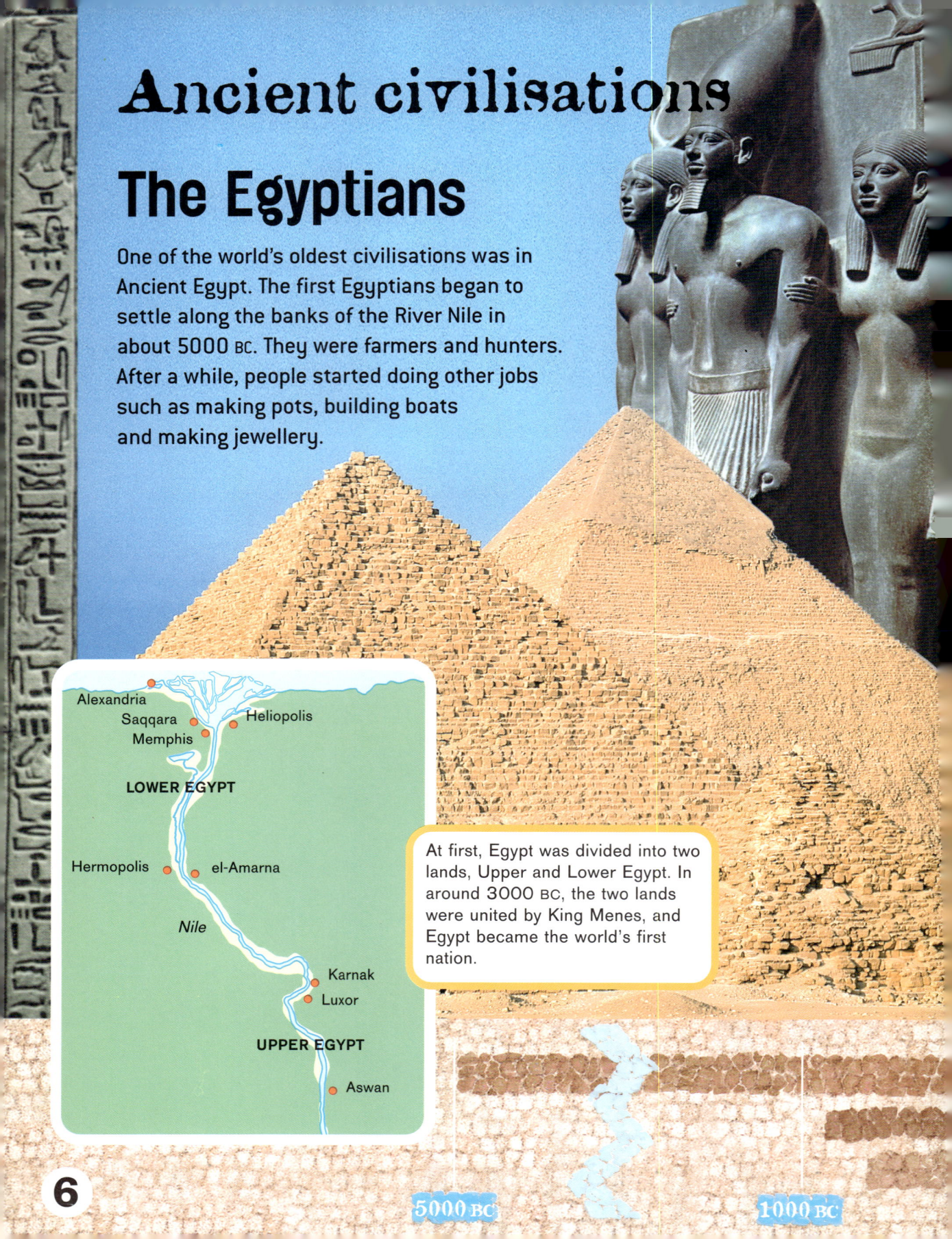

Ancient civilisations

The Egyptians

One of the world's oldest civilisations was in Ancient Egypt. The first Egyptians began to settle along the banks of the River Nile in about 5000 BC. They were farmers and hunters. After a while, people started doing other jobs such as making pots, building boats and making jewellery.

At first, Egypt was divided into two lands, Upper and Lower Egypt. In around 3000 BC, the two lands were united by King Menes, and Egypt became the world's first nation.

Map labels: Alexandria, Saqqara, Memphis, Heliopolis, LOWER EGYPT, Hermopolis, el-Amarna, Nile, Karnak, Luxor, UPPER EGYPT, Aswan

5000 BC · 1000 BC

The Greeks

People have lived in Greece since the Stone Age. But the Ancient Greek civilisation really began in about 2000 BC, when large numbers of people began to settle there. Cities began to form across Greece, and the people thought of themselves as all belonging to one country. They called themselves Hellenes, and their country Hellas. These names are still used today.

The Ancient Greeks founded new cities all around the Mediterranean Sea. The orange areas on this map show the Greek Empire at its largest, in about 300 BC.

The Romans

The Roman Empire was one of the most powerful civilisations in history. In about 700 BC, Rome was just a small Italian town. It soon grew into a huge city, and its armies conquered many countries. By the second century AD, the Roman Empire had spread to many countries around the Mediterranean Sea. The vast empire covered an area that today contains about 30 countries, including England and Wales.

The Roman Empire spread much further than the Greek Empire. The purple areas on this map show the Roman Empire in about AD 120.

Egyptians
Greeks
Romans

500 BC   0   AD 500

Egyptian necklace

This necklace, made from clay beads, was found in Tutankhamen's tomb.

Materials
* Pasta tubes (small packet)
* Paints
* Felt (34 x 26 cm)
* Thick card (12 x 6 cm)
* Glue
* String or cord (50 cm)
* Beads (optional)

Equipment
* Paintbrush
* White crayon
* Hole punch
* Scissors

The Ancient Egyptians loved jewellery. Both men and women wore necklaces, bracelets and anklets made from semi-precious stones, glass and clay. They wore jewellery not only for decoration but also for protection. Many pieces of jewellery contained magic signs to protect them from evil.

Method

- Paint the pasta tubes and allow to dry.

- Place part A of the template (see page 20) on the felt. Draw round it using the white crayon.

- Place part B on the card and draw round it. Repeat this so you have two shapes. Punch the holes as marked on the template.

- Cut out the shapes from the felt and card.

1

2
- Make the end fittings by painting the card shapes. Allow to dry.
- Lay out the card and felt shapes as shown.
- Glue the end fittings in place.

3
- Work out your design. Start in the middle of one strand of felt and arrange the tubes along it.
- Glue each tube into position.
- Repeat this along the other two felt strands.
- Allow to dry.

4
- Thread a piece of string through each hole. Fasten each piece of string in a loop.
- Extra decorations can be added by threading a few pasta tubes or beads onto the string.

9

Egyptian pyramid

The Egyptians built pyramids as tombs for their kings and queens. Between 2700 and 1640 BC they built more than eighty pyramids along the banks of the Nile. Some pyramids took over twenty years to build. At one time, every worker in the land was involved in building pyramids.

These are the great pyramids at Giza, near Cairo.

Materials
* Card (30 x 18 cm)
* Glue
* Paint
* Paper (large sheet)
* Glitter or sand

Equipment
* Pencil
* Scissors
* Ruler
* Knitting needle
* Paintbrush

Method

- Place the template (see page 20) on the card and draw round it. Cut out the shape.

- Draw the dotted lines marked on the template on the card using the pencil and ruler.

- Score along these lines using the knitting needle (or another sharp object).

1

2

- Bend along the scored lines to form a pyramid shape.
- Glue flap A onto side A.

- Glue the other flaps onto the square. Allow to dry.
- Paint the pyramid. Allow to dry.
- Lightly draw some Egyptian pictures or hieroglyphics on each side of the pyramid.

3

- Paint glue over the pencil lines on one side of the pyramid.
- Place the sheet of paper on the table. Tip glitter or sand over the glued lines. Shake the loose glitter or sand onto the paper so you can use it again.

4

- Repeat on the other sides.

Greek coins

Greek coins were made from gold or silver. Different areas of Ancient Greece produced their own coins, and they were often stamped with the symbol of the area they came from. The other side of the coin often pictured the head of a Greek god.

This coin is stamped with a picture of Pegasus, the mythical winged horse.

Materials
* Plasticene
* Talcum powder
* Air hardening clay
* Gold or silver paint

Equipment
* Rolling pin
* Small plastic toy animal
* Soft paintbrush

Method

- Make a ball of plasticene about the size of a tomato.
- Using the rolling pin, roll it out to make a disc.
- Press the toy firmly into the plasticene.
- Gently pull the toy off the plasticene so it leaves its shape.

1

12

2

- Using the soft paintbrush, gently brush talcum powder over the plasticene mould.
- Make a ball of clay about the same size as the ball of plasticene.
- Flatten the ball of clay until it is slightly smaller than the disc of plasticene.
- Lay the clay on top of the plasticene mould and press it into the mould.

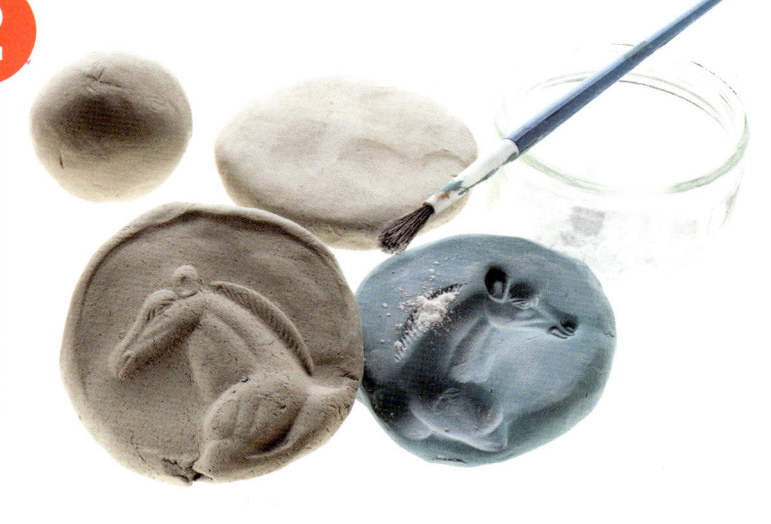

3

- Roll carefully over the top with the rolling pin.
- Carefully pull the clay away from the plasticene, and lay it flat to dry.
- Paint the coins with gold or silver paint.

4

Greek temple photo frame

This picture is of the Temple of Neptune.

The Ancient Greeks believed in many different gods, and built magnificent temples to honour them. They used the best materials and the most skilled craftspeople to make the temples as impressive as possible, because they believed that the gods used the temples as their earthly homes.

Materials
* Card (30 x 22 cm)
* Corrugated paper (14 x 8 cm)
* Sticky tape
* Corrugated cardboard (5 x 5 cm)
* Glue
* Gravel or small stones

Equipment
* Pencil
* Scissors
* Ruler
* Knitting needle

Method

- Place part A of the template (see page 21) on the card and draw round it. Cut out the shape.

- Draw the dotted lines marked on the template on the card using a pencil and ruler.

- Score along these lines using the knitting needle or another sharp object.

- Bend along the scored lines to form the temple shape.

1

- Place part B of the template on the corrugated paper and draw round it. Repeat this so that you have two shapes. Cut out both shapes.

- Make short cuts along both narrow ends of the rectangles.

- Bend each rectangle round to make a tube, and tape along the edge.

- Bend the cut ends of the tubes outwards to make flaps.

2

3

- Place part C of the template on the corrugated cardboard and draw round it. Repeat this so that you have two shapes. Cut out both shapes.

- Spread some glue on the flaps of one end of a column and glue it onto a square. Repeat with the second column. Allow to dry.

- Spread some glue on the top of one square, and glue the column in place inside the temple, making sure that the taped edge is at the back. Repeat with the second column.

4

- Glue the flaps at the base of each column to the bottom of the temple. Allow to dry.

- Spread some glue along the bottom of the temple, making sure you leave a gap at the back for the photo.

- Stick small stones or gravel into the glue.

- Draw a design on the front of the temple if you wish.

- Slip in the photo from the side.

Roman scroll

The Ancient Romans wrote letters and other documents on papyrus scrolls. Papyrus is made from the stem of a plant, and looks a bit like paper. Everything had to be written by hand in Roman times, and people called scribes were employed to keep records of important speeches.

This stone carving shows a teacher reading to his pupils from a scroll.

Materials
* Sugar paper (white or cream)
* Brown paint (or cold tea)
* Piece of bamboo (slightly longer than width of paper)
* Glue
* Ribbon

Equipment
* Large paintbrush
* Pencil
* Felt tip pen

Method

- Tear along the edges of the sugar paper to make them look ragged.

- Paint both sides of the sugar paper with watery brown paint (or cold tea).

1

2
- Glue the bamboo along the narrow edge of the paper.

3
- Write a poem or a letter on the scroll with a pencil.
- Go over the pencil lines with a felt tip pen.

4
- Roll up the scroll and tie it with the ribbon.

Roman mosaic draughts board

This mosaic picture shows three men playing a board game.

The Romans enjoyed playing games. A popular place to play games was in the public baths, where people gathered not only to get clean but also to exercise and meet other people. Some people played ball games or wrestled. Others preferred less energetic board games.

Materials
* Thick card (30 x 30 cm)
* Black or coloured paper (40 x 40 cm)
* Glue
* Old magazines
* Air hardening clay
* Paint

Equipment
* Scissors
* Pencil
* Paintbrush

Method

To make the board

- Spread some glue on one side of the card. Place the card, glue side down, roughly in the centre of the paper.

- Cut off the corners of the paper up to the corners of the card. Glue the edges of the paper down onto the card.

2

- Trace or copy the template (see page 22) onto the board.

- Choose two colours. In the old magazines, find pictures with these colours in.

- Cut out squares from the pictures. The squares should be slightly smaller than the squares on the board.

- Glue the squares onto the board.

To make the counters

- Roll the clay into 24 small balls, then flatten the balls into disc shapes. Allow to dry.

- Paint 12 counters one colour and 12 the other colour.

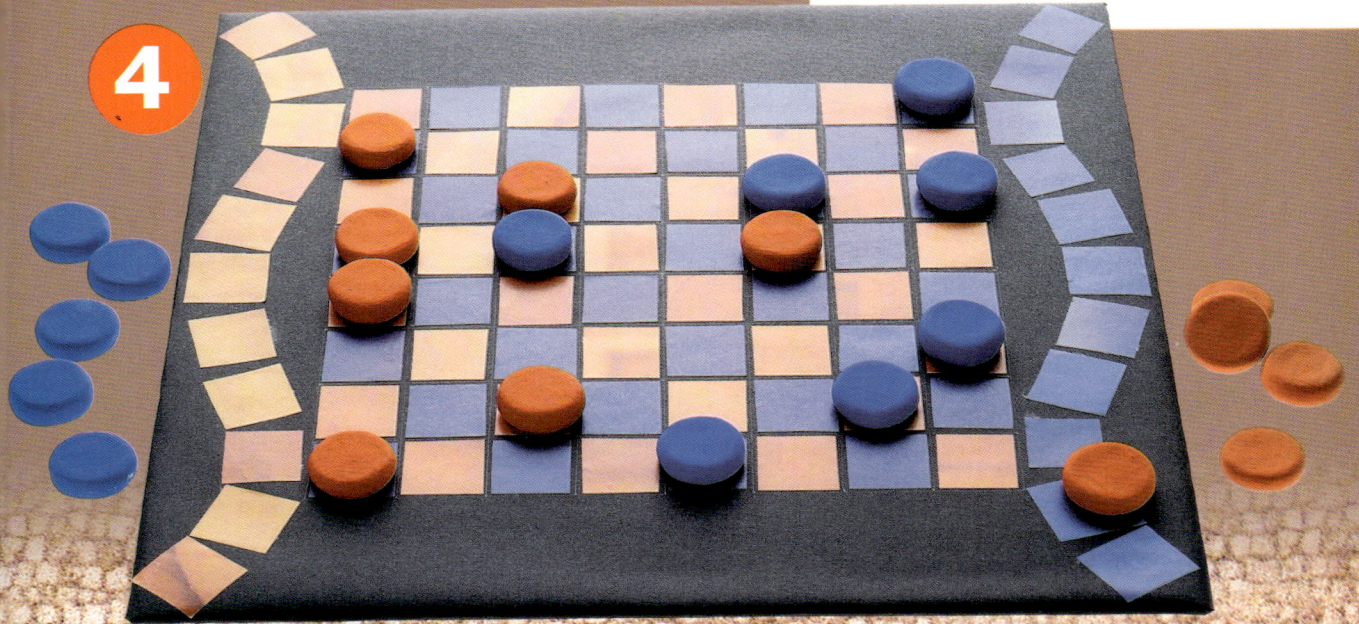

3

4

19

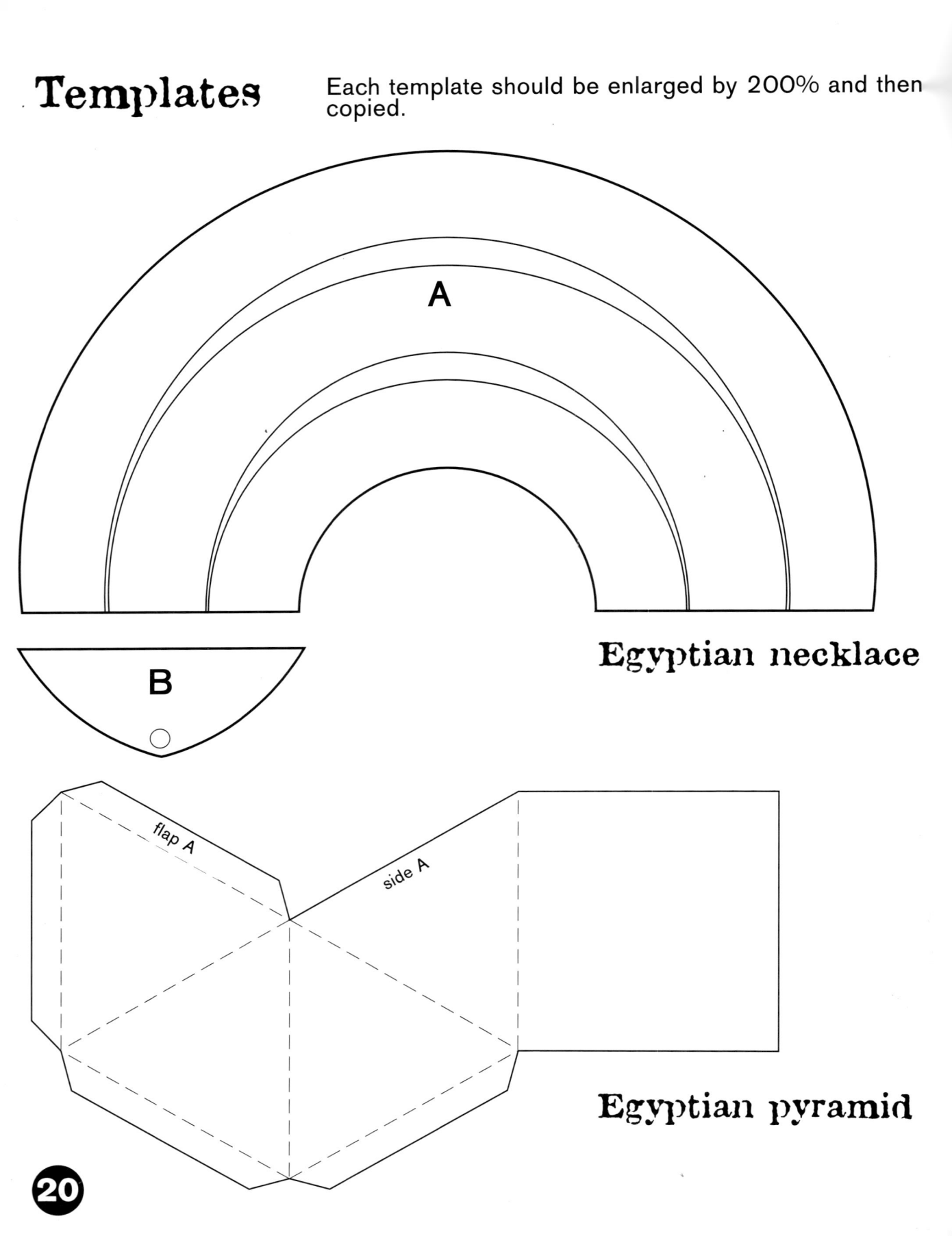

Templates

Each template should be enlarged by 200% and then copied.

A

B

Egyptian necklace

flap A

side A

Egyptian pyramid

Greek temple
photo frame

C

B

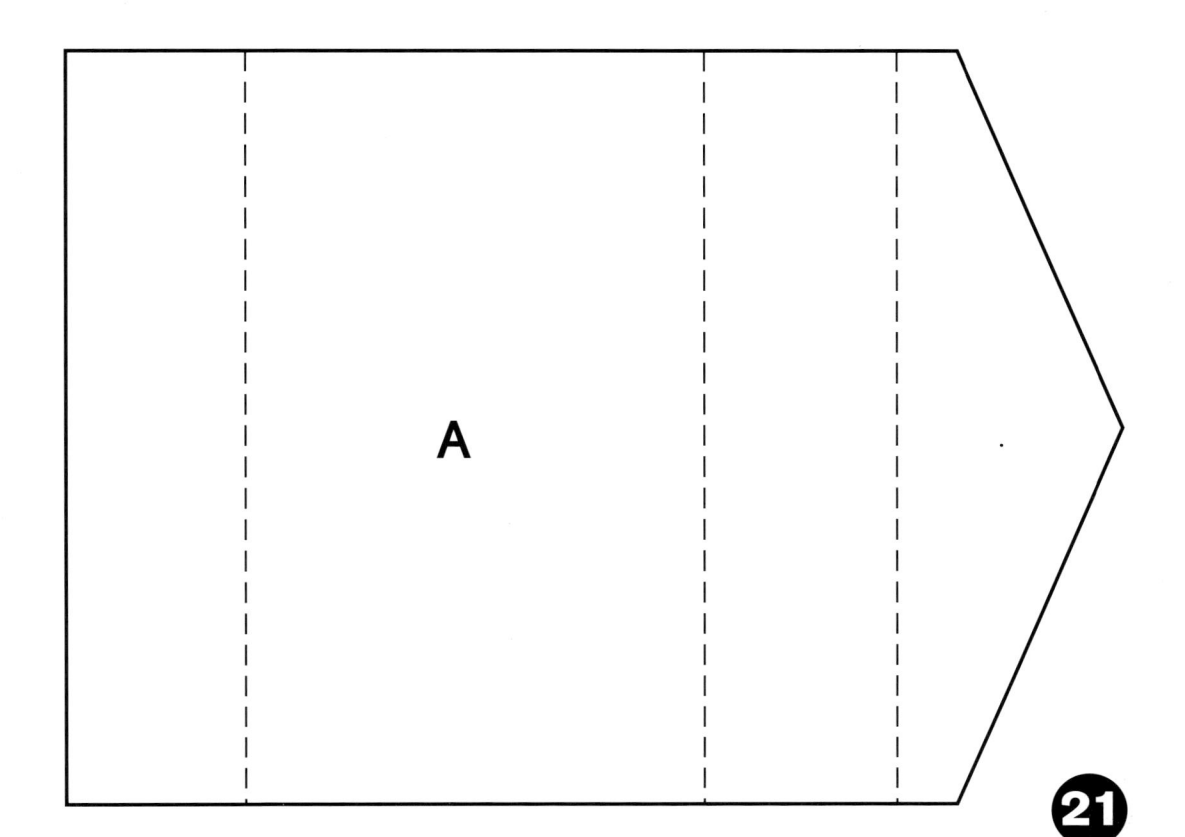

A

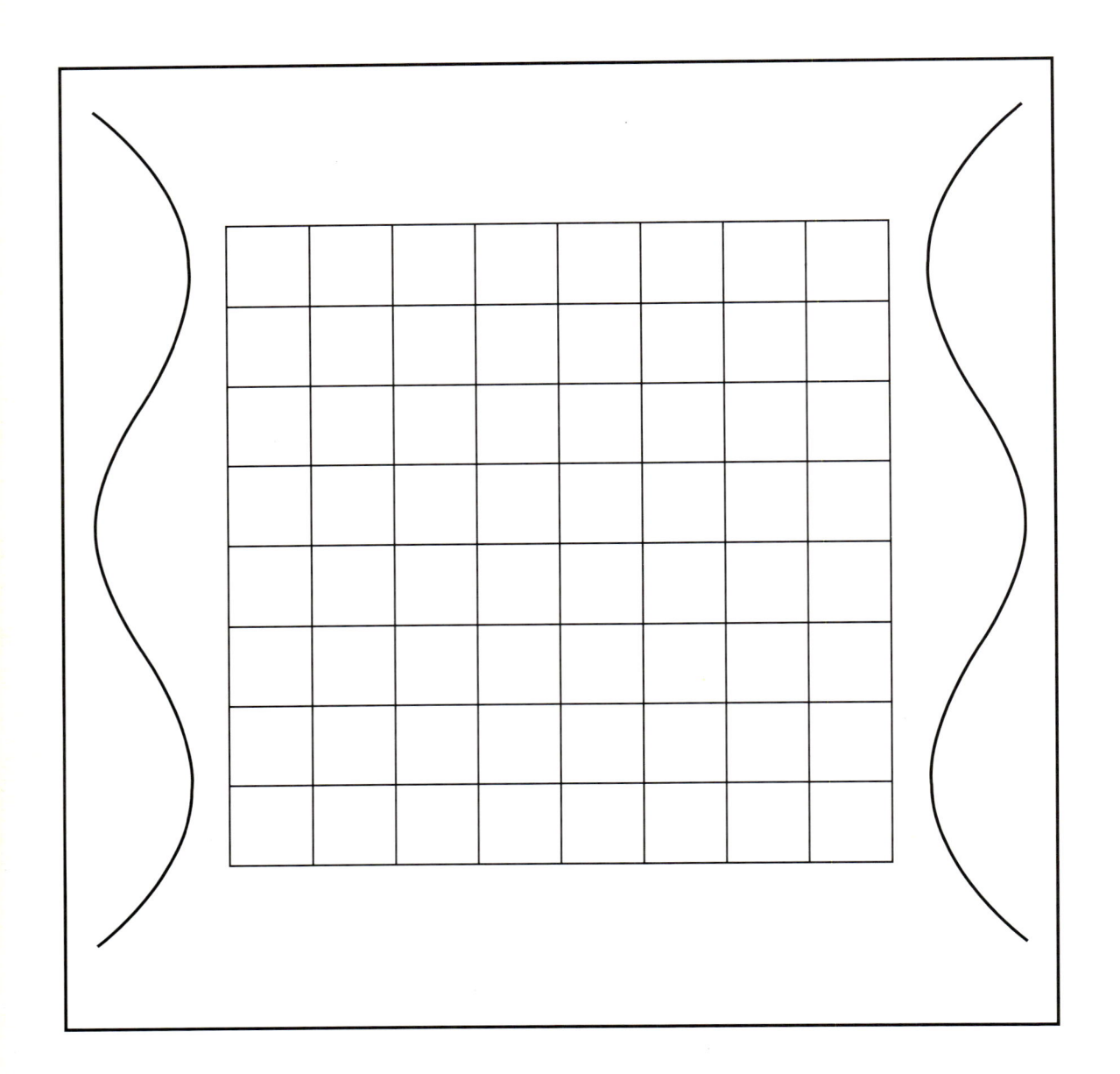

Roman mosaic draughts board

Bibliography

Title	Author	Publisher
Craft Topics: Romans	N. Baxter	Franklin Watts
Art from the Past: The Egyptians	Gillian Chapman	Heinemann
Crafts from the Past: The Greeks	Gillian Chapman	Heinemann
Crafts from the Past: The Romans	Gillian Chapman	Heinemann
The Ancient Greeks Activity Book	Jenny Chattington	British Museum Press
The Ancient Romans Activity Book	Ralph Jackson & Simon James	British Museum Press
The Ancient Egyptian Activity Book	Lise Manniche	British Museum Press
Craft Topics: Greeks	Ruth Thomson	Franklin Watts
Craft Topics: Egyptians	Rachael Wright	Franklin Watts

Index

artefact 4

artists 4

baths 18

civilisation 4, 6, 7

coin 12, 13

craftspeople 4, 14

Egypt 6

Egyptian 4, 6, 7, 8, 10, 11, 20, 23

games 18

Giza 10

gods 12, 14

Greece 7, 12

Greek 4, 7, 12, 14, 21, 23

Hellas 7

Hellenes 7

jewellery 6, 8

Mediterranean Sea 7

Menes, King 6

mosaic 18, 22

necklace 8, 20

Nile, the 6, 10

papyrus 16

Pegasus 12

pottery 4

Roman 4, 7, 16, 18, 22, 23

Rome 7

scribe 16

scroll 16, 17

temple 14, 15, 21

Tutankhamen 8